A Note to Parents

DK READERS is a compelling program for beginning readers, designed in conjunction with leading literacy experts, including Dr. Linda Gambrell, Distinguished Professor of Education at Clemson University. Dr. Gambrell has served as President of the National Reading Conference, the College Reading Association, and the International Reading Association.

Beautiful illustrations and superb full-color photographs combine with engaging, easy-to-read stories to offer a fresh approach to each subject in the series. Each DK READER is guaranteed to capture a child's interest while developing his or her reading skills, general knowledge, and love of reading.

The five levels of DK READERS are aimed at different reading abilities, enabling you to choose the books that are exactly right for your child:

Pre-level 1: Learning to read
Level 1: Beginning to read
Level 2: Beginning to read alone
Level 3: Reading alone
Level 4: Proficient readers

The "normal" age at which a child begins to read can be anywhere from three to eight years old. Adult participation through the lower levels is very helpful for providing encouragement, discussing storylines, and sounding out unfamiliar words.

No matter which level you select, you can be sure that you are helping your child learn to read, then read to learn!

Project Editor Louise Pritchard
Art Editor Jill Plank
US Editor Regina Kahney
Production Siu Chan
Picture Researcher Liz Moore
Jacket Designer Natalie Godwin
Illustrator Peter Dennis
Publishing Manager Bridget Giles

Reading Consultant
Linda B. Gambrell

First American edition, 2000
This edition, 2010
18 10 9 8 7 6 5
022-177254-Mar/2010
Published in the United States by DK Publishing
345 Hudson Street, New York, New York 10014

Published in Great Britain by Dorling Kindersley Limited

DK books are available at special discounts when purchased
in bulk for sales promotions, premiums, fund-raising,
or educational use.

For details, contact: DK Publishing Special Markets
345 Hudson Street, New York, New York 10014
SpecialSales@dk.com

A catalog record for this book is available
from the Library of Congress

ISBN: 978-0-7566-5880-9 (pb)
ISBN: 978-0-7566-5881-6 (plc)

Color reproduction by Colourscan, Singapore
Printed and bound in China

The publisher would like to thank the following for
their kind permission to reproduce their photographs:
Key: c=center; t=top; b=bottom; l=left; r=right
National Geographic Image Collection: Chris Johns 26–27b;
NOAA Photo Library/NOAA Central Library (www.photolib.noaa.
gov/): 28t, 30; **Planet Earth Pictures**: Alex Benwell 15br, Paolo
Fanciulli 7br; **Robert Harding Picture Library**: 16, Sheila
Beougher 18bl, Warren Faidley/Agliolo 1br, Warren Faidley/Int'l
Stock 16–17, 18tr, Jeff Greenberg 22tr; **Tony Stone Images**: 21tr,
Christoph Burki 5tr, Jerry Kobalenko 4–5, John Lund 32, Alan R
Moller 19b, Camille Tokerud 15cr; **Topham Picturepoint**:
25br, J. McTyre 24.
Jacket images: *Front*: Getty Images: Paul & Lindamarie Ambrose

A WORLD OF IDEAS:
SEE ALL THERE IS TO KNOW

www.dk.com

DK READERS

BEGINNING TO READ ALONE

2

Twisters!

Written by Kate Hayden

DK

Rob was working
in his farmyard in Texas.
It was a peaceful spring day.
But his dog, Barney, was unhappy.
He hid under a tractor
and would not come out.
Rob wondered if Barney was ill.

Second sense

Animals have sharper senses than we have. Many can sense changes in the weather, like just before a bad storm.

Suddenly the sky went dark.
Hailstones as big as golf balls
pelted down from the sky.
Thunder rolled
and lightning flashed.
Then came a deathly stillness
in the air.
Somehow, Barney had known!

A moment later,
huge black clouds began to spin.
They bubbled at the top
like boiling milk.
Gusts of wind blew straw around.
Just then, a finger of cloud
spiraled down from the sky.
A twister!

Rob stood rooted to the spot.

The twister touched the ground.

Mud and grass swirled up

like smoke from a bonfire.

That was only the start.

The twister began to move.

It skipped and bounced

across the fields.

It grew bigger, faster, and dirtier

as it picked up mud

from the ground.

Waterspouts

Twisters out at sea
are called waterspouts.
They whisk up water.
The tallest one ever seen
was 1 mile (1.6 km) high.

Rob watched in horror
as the twister went
toward his neighbor's farm.
It picked up straw, trees—
and even a farm truck.
It spun them around in its funnel.

Rob sighed with relief when
the twister moved away.
He thought he was safe.
But then the twister
changed direction—
right toward him!

Suddenly the twister was hanging
right over Rob's farm.
There was a noise
like a rushing waterfall,
then—BANG!
The barn exploded
as if a bomb had gone off inside it.

Rob ran with Barney
to the cellar in his house.
His ears were hurting
and he could hardly breathe.
That's because the air pressure
inside a twister is very low.
This makes people's ears ache
and causes buildings to explode.

Just as Rob reached
the cellar,
his front porch flew off
with an ear-splitting CRASH!
Then came a SMASH
as the house windows blew in.
Two minutes later, all was silent.

Rob came up from the cellar.
Furniture lay smashed on the floor.
Most of the doors
and windows were gone.
Rob felt lucky
to be alive.

Neighbors helped Rob clean up.
The twister did not damage
the neighbors' house.

Warm air

Cold air

Twisters can form
when cold air meets warm air.
The warm air is sucked up
in a swirling column
called a funnel cloud.
It spins at great speed.
Twisters contain
the most deadly winds
in the world.

No one knows
what a twister will do next.
It can lift up a large truck
and smash it to pieces,
but leave small objects undamaged.

A twister once picked up a baby
and set him down safely
300 ft (90 m) away.
The baby did not
even wake up!

Strange showers
When twisters drop
things they've picked up,
strange things can happen.
A twister in England
caused a shower of frogs.

There are lots of
strange stories
about twisters.
A twister once
blew away
a man's
birth certificate.
The twister carried it
50 miles (80 kilometers)
then dropped it
in a friend's garden.
Another twister
sucked up some roses
and water from a vase.
It dropped them in another room.
But it left the vase on the table.

One twister picked up
a jar of pickles
and carried the jar for miles
(kilometers) without damaging it.

Twisters come in many different shapes and sizes. They can be thin, white, and wispy. Or they can be big, thick, and black.

They can even be in color! If a twister travels across a muddy field, the mud turns it brown— and very smelly!

Twisters can grow bigger and faster
as they go along.
Some look like they have
a loop or knot in the middle.
Some are wider at the bottom
than at the top.
Some are shaped like a tube.
Others look like a slice of pie.

Lots of people
have seen a twister
from the outside.
But only a few have looked
inside a twister and survived.

A farmer named Will Keller
once looked up into a twister
from his underground shelter.
Just as he closed
the door of his shelter,
he saw lots of mini twisters
inside the big twister.
These mini twisters can rip
through a building
and slice it to shreds.

Twister speeds

Some twisters travel
only as fast as
a person walking.
Others travel
as fast as express trains.

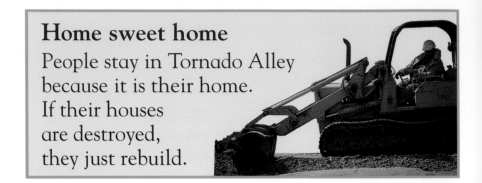

Home sweet home
People stay in Tornado Alley
because it is their home.
If their houses
are destroyed,
they just rebuild.

Twisters are
also known
as tornados.
There is an area
in the U.S.
that is called
Tornado Alley.
It is famous for
its deadly twisters.
Up to 300 occur there
every year between April and July.
They kill more than 80 people.

Twisters form during these months
as warm air from the south meets
cold air from the north—
right over Tornado Alley.

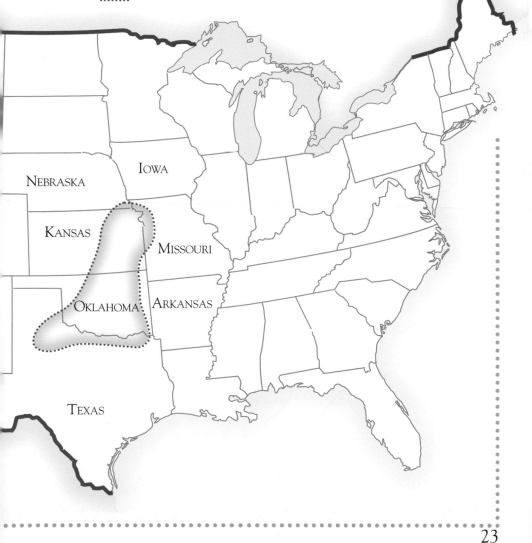

☐☐☐ TORNADO ALLEY

NEBRASKA

IOWA

KANSAS

MISSOURI

OKLAHOMA ARKANSAS

TEXAS

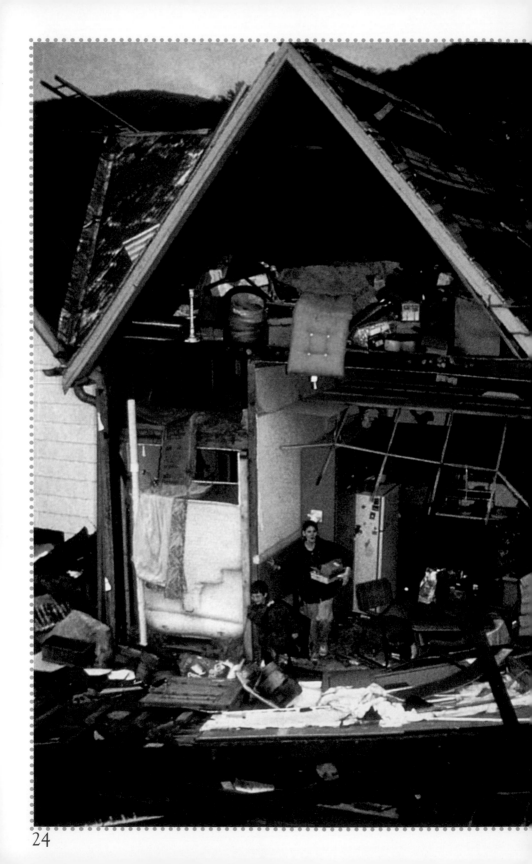

Twisters are graded from 0 to 5
on a scale called the Fujita Scale.
An F0 damages chimneys.
An F1 snaps telephone poles.
An F2 rips off roofs.
An F3 flips over trains.
An F4 destroys even strong homes.
An F5 leaves few things standing.
In 1999, an F5 ripped through
Oklahoma City, Oklahoma.
It killed 45 people.

The worst twister
In 1925, one twister
in Tornado Alley
destroyed four towns
in less than four hours.
It killed 689 people.

People in Tornado Alley are well prepared for twisters. Most of them have an underground shelter outside their home.

Emergency supplies
People keep
emergency supplies
in their shelters—
food, drink, flashlights,
and a first-aid kit.

Some people in Texas have
a fiberglass shelter
buried in their backyard.

People without
a shelter hide
in a cellar
or small room
in the middle
of their house.

*The Malone family
next to their
fiberglass shelter
before it is buried*

Gary England is
a TV weather reporter
in Oklahoma City.
When lots of twisters
are expected,
Gary's team stays on the air
for 30 hours or more.

Scientists tell Gary
what the weather will be.
Gary can then tell viewers.
The scientists use a computer
to help them forecast twisters.
The computer makes a picture
that shows where a twister is
and how fast it is traveling.

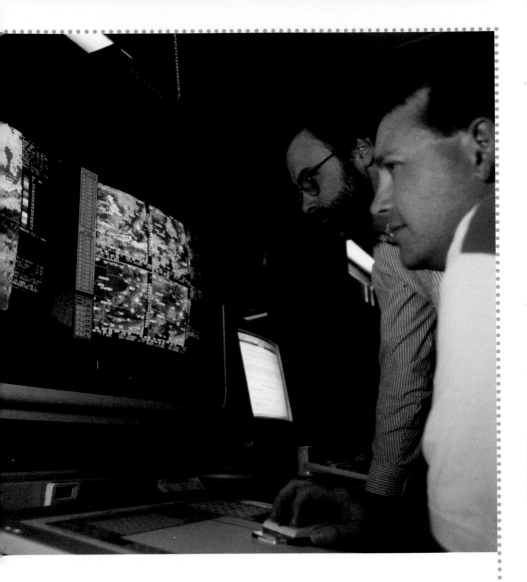

Forecasts from space

Spacecraft called satellites
orbit around Earth.
Some send information
about the weather
to scientists on Earth.

The scientists can tell Gary
what they think will happen.
But storm trackers on the road
know what is actually happening.
These people risk their lives
to find and follow twisters.
Many of them have
modern equipment
such as a satellite dish.

The trackers tell Gary
all about a twister—
where it is
and where it is going.
They can even tell him
when a twister is brewing.

In the past, people did not know when a twister was coming. Today, the trackers and scientists give people time to find shelter, and hundreds of lives are saved.

A storm tracker's modern truck

Twister facts

People in Tornado Alley
can check for twisters
when they fill their cars
with gasoline.
Many pumps show
the weather forecast
on a screen.

Winds inside a twister
can spin around at up to
300 miles (500 km) per hour.

In April 1974,
148 tornados tore through
13 states in the U.S.
Six of them were F5s—
the strongest type of tornado.

In 1994, in Australia,
hundreds of fish fell
from the sky.
This was probably
the work of a twister.

Twisters that suck up
sand in deserts
are called dust devils.

A twister can last
for any length of time—
from a few minutes
to an hour.